T0105262

Books by James Schuyler

Poems

Freely Espousing
The Crystal Lithium
Hymn to Life
The Morning of the Poem

Novels

Alfred and Guinevere
A Nest of Ninnies (with John Ashbery)
What's for Dinner?

Prose and Poems

The Home Book (edited by Trevor Winkfield)

The Morning of the Poem

P O E M S   B Y

JAMES SCHUYLER

Farrar, Straus and Giroux • New York

THE
MORNING
OF THE
POEM

Printed in the United States of America
Designed by Cynthia Krupat
First edition, 1980
Some of these poems first appeared in
The New Yorker, The New York Review of
Books, Parenthese, Poetry, and *The Times*
Literary Supplement

For Darragh Park

Contents

New Poems

This Dark Apartment / 3
June 30, 1974 / 5
Korean Mums / 9
Growing Dark / 11
Dec. 28, 1974 / 13
Good Morning / 15
Song / 17
A Name Day / 18
Footnote / 21
Afterward / 22
I Sit Down to Type / 24
The Snow / 27
Wystan Auden / 28
Dining Out with Doug and Frank / 31

The Payne Whitney Poems

Trip / 43
We Walk / 44
Arches / 45
Linen / 46
Heather and Calendulas / 47
Back / 48
Blizzard / 49

February 13, 1975 / 50
Sleep / 51
Pastime / 52
What / 53

The Morning of the Poem

The Morning of the Poem / 57

NEW
POEMS

This Dark Apartment

Coming from the deli
a block away today I
saw the UN building
shine and in all the
months and years I've
lived in this apartment
I took so you and I
would have a place to
meet I never noticed
that it was in my view.

I remember very well
the morning I walked in
and found you in bed
with X. He dressed
and left. You dressed
too. I said, "Stay
five minutes." You
did. You said, "That's
the way it is." It
was not much of a surprise.

Then X got on speed
and ripped off an
antique chest and an
air conditioner, etc.
After he was gone and

you had changed the
Segal lock, I asked
you on the phone, "Can't
you be content with
your wife and me?" "I'm
not built that way,"
you said. No surprise.

Now, without saying
why, you've let me go.
You don't return my
calls, who used to call
me almost every evening
when I lived in the coun-
try. "Hasn't he told you
why?" "No, and I doubt he
ever will." Goodbye. It's
mysterious and frustrating.

How I wish you would come
back! I could tell
you how, when I lived
on East 49th, first
with Frank and then with John,
we had a lovely view of
the UN building and the
Beekman Towers. They were
not my lovers, though.
You were. You said so.

June 30, 1974

[*For Jane and Joe Hazan*]

Let me tell you
that this weekend Sunday
morning in the country
fills my soul
with tranquil joy:
the dunes beyond
the pond beyond
the humps of bayberry—
my favorite
shrub (today,
at least)—are
silent as a mountain
range: such a
subtle profile
against a sky that
goes from dawn
to blue. The roses
stir, the grapevine
at one end of the deck
shakes and turns
its youngest leaves
so they show pale
and flower-like.
A redwing blackbird
pecks at the grass;
another perches on a bush.

Another way, a millionaire's
white château turns
its flank to catch
the risen sun. No
other houses, except
this charming one,
alive with paintings,
plants and quiet.
I haven't said
a word. I like
to be alone
with friends. To get up
to this morning view
and eat poached eggs
and extra toast with
Tiptree Gooseberry Preserve
(green)—and coffee,
milk, no sugar. Jane
said she heard
the freeze-dried kind
is healthier when
we went shopping
yesterday and she
and John bought
crude blue Persian plates.
How can coffee be
healthful? I mused
as sunny wind
streamed in the car
window driving home.

Home! How lucky to
have one, how arduous
to make this scene
of beauty for
your family and
friends. Friends!
How we must have
sounded, gossiping at
the dinner table
last night. Why, *that*
dinner table is
this breakfast table:
"The boy in trousers
is not the same boy
in no trousers," who
said? Discontinuity
in all we see and are:
the same, yet change,
change, change. "Inez,
it's good to see you."
Here comes the cat, sedate,
that killed and brought
a goldfinch yesterday.
I'd like to go out
for a swim but
it's a little cool
for that. Enough to
sit here drinking coffee,
writing, watching the clear
day ripen (such

a rainy June we had)
while Jane and Joe
sleep in their room
and John in his. I
think I'll make more toast.

Korean Mums

beside me in this garden
are huge and daisy-like
(why not? are not
oxeye daisies a chrysanthemum?),
shrubby and thick-stalked,
the leaves pointing up
the stems from which
the flowers burst in
sunbursts. I love
this garden in all its moods,
even under its winter coat
of salt hay, or now,
in October, more than
half gone over: here
a rose, there a clump
of aconite. This morning
one of the dogs killed
a barn owl. Bob saw
it happen, tried to
intervene. The Airedale
snapped its neck and left
it lying. Now the bird
lies buried by an apple
tree. Last evening
from the table we saw
the owl, huge in the dusk,
circling the field

on owl-silent wings.
The first one ever seen
here: now it's gone,
a dream you just remember.

The dogs are barking. In
the studio music plays
and Bob and Darragh paint.
I sit scribbling in a little
notebook at a garden table,
too hot in a heavy shirt
in the mid-October sun
into which the Korean mums
all face. There is a
dull book with me,
an apple core, cigarettes,
an ashtray. Behind me
the rue I gave Bob
flourishes. Light on leaves,
so much to see, and
all I really see is that
owl, its bulk troubling
the twilight. I'll
soon forget it: what
is there I have not forgot?
Or one day will forget:
this garden, the breeze
in stillness, even
the words, Korean mums.

Growing Dark

The grass shakes.
Smoke streaks, no,
cloud strokes.
The dogs are fed.
Their licenses
clank on pottery.
The phone rings.
And is answered.
The pond path
is washed-out grass
between green
winter cover.
Last night in
bed I read.
You came to
my room and
said, "Isn't
the world
terrible?" "My
dear . . ." I
said. It could be
and has been
worse. So
beautiful and
things keep getting
in between. When
I was young I

hurt others. Now,
others have hurt
me. In the night
I thought I heard
a dog bark.
Racking sobs.
Poor guy. Yet,
I got my sleep.

Dec. 28, 1974

The plants against the light
which shines in (it's four o'clock)
right on my chair: I'm in my chair:
are silhouettes, barely green,
growing black as my eyes move right,
right to where the sun is.
I am blinded by a firey circle:
I can't see what I write. A man
comes down iron stairs (I
don't look up) and picks up brushes
which, against a sonata of Scriabin's,
rattle like wind in a bamboo clump.
A wooden sound, and purposeful footsteps
softened by a drop-cloth-covered floor.
To be encubed in flaming splendor,
one foot on a Chinese rug, while
the mad emotive music
tears at my heart. Rip it open:
I want to cleanse it in an icy wind.
And what kind of tripe is that?
Still, last night I did wish—
no, that's my business and I
don't wish it now. "Your poems,"
a clunkhead said, "have grown
more open." I don't want to be open,
merely to say, to see and say, things
as they are. That at my elbow

there is a wicker table. *Hortus*
Second says a book. The fields
beyond the feeding sparrows are
brown, palely brown yet with an inward glow
like that of someone of a frank good nature
whom you trust. I want to hear the music
hanging in the air and drink my
Coca-Cola. The sun is off me now,
the sky begins to color up, the air
in here is filled with wildly flying notes.
Yes, the sun moves off to the right
and prepares to sink, setting,
beyond the dunes, an ocean on fire.

Good Morning

morning, or heartache. In
the night it rained
it misted. The walks
are dark with it, the grass
is thick with it. In
resignation I
doff my walking shorts,
put on elephant hide,
or Levi's. Bitter coffee.

Rae turns to me and
speaks her rage
but gently as a gentle
woman would. The night
nurse means well, is
something else jabbering
loudly in the hall
at night. An over-
ripe banana. I
have yet to learn
to speak my rage.

Where I go books
pile up. Constable's
letters, Balzac,
Afternoon Men. It's
cool enough to

shut the window. So
I do. Silver day
how shall I polish you?

Song

The light lies layered in the leaves.
Trees, and trees, more trees.
A cloud boy brings the evening paper:
The Evening Sun. It sets.
Not sharply or at once
a stately progress down the sky
(it's gilt and pink and faintly green)
above, beyond, behind the evening leaves
of trees. Traffic sounds and
bells resound in silver clangs
the hour, a tune, my friend
Pierrot. The violet hour:
the grass is violent green.
A weeping beech is gray,
a copper beech is copper red.
Tennis nets hang
unused in unused stillness.
A car starts up and
whispers into what will soon be night.
A tennis ball is served.
A horsefly vanishes.
A smoking cigarette.
A day (so many and so few)
dies down a hardened sky
and leaves are lap-held notebook leaves
discriminated barely
in light no longer layered.

A Name Day

[*For Anne Dunn*]

You know da Vinci's painting of
The Virgin sitting in her mother's lap,
Bending and reaching toward the child:
Mary, Jesus, and St. Anne: beautiful
Names: Anne, from a Latin name from
The Hebrew name Hannah. The sun shines
Here and out the window I see green, green
Cut into myriad shapes, a bare-foot-
Caressing carpet of fresh-mown grass (a
Gift from Persia, courtesy of D. Kermani),
Green chopped into various leaves: walnut, maple,
Privet, Solomon's-seal, needles of spruce:
Green with evening sunlight on it,
Green going deep into penetrable shade:
What is that one red leaf? It's too
Soon, it's only late July. I'm frightened,
Anne, my mother, who is eighty-six, just
A few minutes ago had some kind of slight
Attack. I held her and said, "Put your weight
On me, put your weight on me." She said,
"I can't stand it." She won't let me
Call a doctor: my brother and his wife
Are out of town: they know better than I
How to handle her. I think—I hope—I
Pray, that it was just an arthritic spasm.

Beneficent St. Anne, look down and
Protect us. Mary, sustain us in our need.

Here it is all so beautiful and green:
There where you are it is night, big
Stars, perhaps: do candles flare as
You and yours gather to celebrate
Your name day, there in pungent Provence?
What would I like to give you?
Beads, a steel rose, a book?
No, flowers, roses, real roses
—Maréchal Niel, Gloire de
Dijon, Variegata di Bologna,
Madame Alfred Carrière, Souvenir
de la Malmaison, Georg Arends,
Prince Camille de Rohan: or,
Maybe better, homelier,
Canadian columbine, rusty red
(Or rather orange?), spurred,
Hanging down, drying, turning
Brown, turning up, a cup
Full of fine black seeds
That sparkle, wake-robin,
Trillium, a dish of rich
Soft moss stuck with little
Flowers from the woods—
Bloodroot, perhaps
Rose pogonia, sea lavender
And, best of all, bunches
And bunches and bunches of

New England asters, not blue,
Not violet, certainly not
Purple: bright-yellow-
Centered, so many crowded
Into vases and bowls that
The house seems awash
With sea and sun. (My
Mother is better: I hear
Her cooking supper: the throbbing
Of my heart slows down.) I
Wish I were there with you,
Gathered with friends
And family, to celebrate
Your name day, Anne. (Along
With the flowers, I send
You a New Brunswick lobster.)

Footnote

The bluet is a small flower, creamy-throated, that grows in patches in New England lawns. The bluet (French pronunciation) is the shaggy cornflower, growing wild in France. "The Bluet" is a poem I wrote. *The Bluet* is a painting of Joan Mitchell's. The thick hard blue runs and holds. All of them, broken-up pieces of sky, hard sky, soft sky. Today I'll take Joan's giant vision, running and holding, staring you down with beauty. Though I need reject none. Bluet. "Bloo-ay."

Afterward

is much as before. Night
slams gently down. I cannot
open this container: and
do and the pills all lie
"star-scattered on" the
rug, which by mischance is
the color of the pills. Do
you ever swear out loud
when you're alone? I do
and did, like that painting,
The Gleaners. The yellow
lamp spreads a friendly glow
on my new Olivetti and
on me. I'm drinking
Diet Pepsi. The ulnar
nerve in my right arm got
pinched I don't know how
and my little finger is
numb: a drag when typing.
The past ten months
were something else:
pneumonia, diabetes, a
fire in bed (*extase, cauchemar,
sommeil dans un nid de flammes*),
months getting skin
grafts for third-degree
burns (for laughs, try

sleeping in an airplane
splint) and getting
poisoned by the side
effects of a potent
tranquilizer: it took
two more months to
learn to walk again
and when I came out
feeling great wham
a nervous breakdown: four
weeks in another hospital.
St. Vincent's, the Neurological
Institute, Tower Nine at
Roosevelt: "You've had too
many hospitals," my doctor
said, "I'm going to get you
out of here as fast as I
can," and so he did. It's
funny to be free again: to
look out and see
the gorgeous October day
and know that I
can stroll right out into
it and for as long as
I wish and that's what I
do. This room needs flowers.

I Sit Down to Type

So long postponed, so near at hand.
—WALLACE STEVENS

and arise whatever for?
SUGAR FREE! SUGAR FREE! TAB.
My window faces west. I mean south.
I push it up and, in
the guise of sunbeams,
God floods my room.
He's in one of his
less malevolent moods.
But God? I don't believe
in God: not for myself,
I mean. For others, it's
another story: at least
one of my friends has
a guardian angel, and
a Jesuit priest I will
call "Father Bill" is
going to heaven. Such
goodness cannot possibly
go unrewarded. But me?
I'm worm food. Someone
beautiful once asked
about religion and I said,
"I'm a crypto-Catholic."
"I'm not sure what you
mean." "Me either." In

fact, I am a Presbyterian:
but before I was
confirmed I'd read
Of Human Bondage
(if that phone rings
one more time I am
going to castrate it
with nail scissors)
and became an atheist:
imagine it: losing your
faith because of a book
by one of the most over-
rated writers of all time.
"There's this watch, see,
and where there's a watch—"
Yawn. I have a scab:
this proves there is a devil
clad in bright red
long johns. In our more
intimate moments I
call him "Sweetie Pie."
And yet I am religious: I
believe implacably in
the perfectibility of man:
to me, we are at the crux,
the most exciting moment
in the history of man:
an X ray of a brain, prisons
transposed to hospitals,
the dawning of the realization

that all men are born creative
(Kenneth Koch
could teach a golf ball
how to write pantoums),
and so on: needless to
say, this is not going
to happen in my time—
nor in yours, baby.
When I was four someone
named Mabel took me to mass:
a gray church on a gray day.
I had a vision: the first
of many. We went home and
my father said, "Did the
priest come riding in on
his ass?" "Why, Mark,"
my mother stated. Ever since
that gray vision—no
matter what I say, no
matter what I think I think—
it has been my profoundest
prayer that God will grant
me grace and I will die
a Catholic, secure in his
all-forgiving love.

The Snow

that fell and iced
the walks and streets
is melted off: it's
gone. I slipped a
little as I strode.
It's early winter
yet though, more and
much is yet to come.
This gray day though
is much too warm
for snow. The window's
up a crack and I shiver
only slightly. I
think of you and then
my thought slides
on, like slipping
on a lightly iced
walk. I have no more
poems for you, chum,
only for the ice and snow.

Wystan Auden

I went to his fortieth birthday
party: was it really twenty-seven
years ago? I don't remember what
street he was living on, but he
was adapting *The Duchess of Malfi*
for the modern stage, in which
Canada Lee appeared in white face:
it was that long ago. It was in
that apartment I just missed
meeting Brecht and T. S. Eliot.

I remember Chester so often saying,
"Oh *Wystan!*" while Wystan looked
pleased at having stirred him up.

On Ischia he claimed to take
St. Restituta seriously, and
sat at Maria's café in the cobbled
square saying, "Poets should
dress like businessmen," while
he wore an incredible peach-
colored nylon shirt. And on
Fire Island his telling someone,
"You must write each book as
though it were your last." And
when he learned that in Florence
I and my friend Bill Aalto had

fished his drafts of poems
out of the wastepaper basket,
he took to burning them, saying,
"I feel like an ambassador burning
secret papers." When he got off
the liner at Naples, in black and
a homburg, he said, "I've just
read *all* of Doughty's *The Dawn
in Britain.*" And earlier, right
after the war, "My dear, I'm the
first major poet to have flown
the Atlantic." He was very kind.
Once, when I had an operation
in Rome, he wrote me quite a large
check: I forget for how much.
When I sent it back and asked
for (for a more favorable ex-
change on the black market)
cash, he sent it, along with
a cross note saying he was
a busy man. Once when a group
of us made an excursion from
Ischia—Capri, Sorrento, Positano,
Amalfi, Pompeii—he suddenly
said at cocktails on a pensione
terrace: "More of this sitting
around like beasts!" He was
industrious, writing away in
a smoky room—fug—in a
ledger or on loose sheets

poems, some of which I typed
for him (they're in *Nones*).
I don't have to burn his
letters as he asked his
friends to do: they were lost
a long time ago. So much
to remember, so little to
say: that he liked martinis
and was greedy about the wine?
I always thought he would live
to a great age. He did not.
Wystan, kind man and great poet,
goodbye.

Dining Out with Doug and Frank

[*For Frank Polach*]

Not quite yet. First,
around the corner for a visit
to the Bella Landauer Collection
of printed ephemera:
luscious lithos and why did
Fairy Soap vanish and
Crouch and Fitzgerald survive?
Fairy Soap was once a
household word! I've been living
at Broadway and West 74th
for a week and still haven't
ventured on a stroll in
Central Park, two bizarre blocks
away. (Bizarre is for the ex-
town houses, mixing Byzantine
with Gothic and Queen Anne.)
My abstention from the Park
is for Billy Nichols who went
bird-watching there and, for
his binoculars, got his
head beat in. Streaming blood,
he made it to an avenue
where no cab would pick him up
until one did and at
Roosevelt Hospital he waited
several hours before any

doctor took him in hand. A
year later he was dead. But
I'll make the park: I carry
more cash than I should and
walk the street at night
without feeling scared unless
someone scary passes.

        II
Now it's tomorrow,
as usual. Turned out that
Doug (Douglas Crase, the poet)
had to work (he makes his bread
writing speeches): thirty pages
explaining why Eastman Kodak's
semi-slump (?) is just what
the stockholders ordered. He
looked glum, and declined
a drink. By the by did you know
that John Ashbery's grandfather
was offered an investment-in
when George Eastman founded his
great corporation? He turned it
down. Eastman Kodak will survive.
"Yes" and where would our
John be now? I can't imagine him
any different than he is,
a problem which does not arise,
so I went with Frank (the poet,
he makes his dough as a librarian,

botanical librarian at Rutgers
and as a worker he's a beaver:
up at 5:30, home after 7, but
over striped bass he said he
had begun to see the unwisdom
of his ways and next week will
revert to the seven-hour day
for which he's paid. Good. Time
and energy to write. Poetry
takes it out of you, or you
have to have a surge to bring
to it. Words. So useful and
pleasant) to dine at McFeely's
at West 23rd and Eleventh Avenue
by the West River, which is
the right name for the Hudson
when it bifurcates from
the East River to create
Manhattan "an isle of joy."
Take my word for it, don't
(shall I tell you about my
friend who effectively threw
himself under a train in
the Times Square station?
No. Too tender to touch. In
fact, at the moment I've blocked
out his name. No I haven't:
Peter Kemeny, gifted and tormented
fat man) listen to anyone
else.

III

Oh. At the Battery all
that water becomes the
North River, which seems
to me to make no sense
at all. I always thought
Castle Garden faced Calais.

IV

Peconic Bay scallops, the
tiny, the real ones and cooked
in butter, not breaded and
plunged in deep grease. The food
is good and reasonable (for these
days) but the point is McFeely's
itself—the owner's name or
was it always called that? It's
the bar of the old Terminal Hotel
and someone (McFeely?) has had
the wit to restore it to what
it was: all was there, under
layers of paint and abuse, neglect.
You, perhaps, could put a date
on it: I'll vote for 1881
or the 70's. The ceiling is
florid glass, like the cabbage-rose
runners in the grand old hotels
at Saratoga: when were they built?
The bar is thick and long and

sinuous, virile. Mirrors: are
the decorations on them cut
or etched? I do remember that
above the men's room door the
word Toilet is etched
on a transom. Beautiful lettering,
but nothing to what lurks
within: the three most
splendid urinals I've ever
seen. Like Roman steles. I
don't know what I was going
to say. Yes. Does the Terminal Hotel
itself still function? (Did you
know that "they" sold all the
old mirror glass out of Gage
and Tollner's? Donald Droll has
a fit every time he eats there.)
"Terminal," I surmise, because
the hotel faced the terminal
of the 23rd Street ferry, a
perfect sunset sail to Hoboken
and the yummies of the Clam
Broth House, which, thank God,
still survives. Not many do:
Gage and Tollner's, the Clam Broth House,
McSorleys and now McFeely's. Was
that the most beautiful of the
ferry houses or am I thinking
of Christopher Street? And there
was another uptown that crossed

to Jersey and back but docking
further downtown: it sailed
on two diagonals. And wasn't
there one at 42nd? It couldn't
matter less, they're gone, all
gone and we are left with just
the Staten Island ferry, all
right in its way but how often
do you want to pass Miss Liberty
and see that awesome spiky postcard
view? The river ferryboats were
squat and low like tugs, old
and wooden and handsome, you
were *in* the water, *in* the shipping:
Millay wrote a lovely poem about
it all. I cannot accept their
death, or any other death. Bill
Aalto, my first lover (five tumultuous
years found Bill chasing me around
the kitchen table—in Wystan Auden's
house in Forio d'Ischia—with
a carving knife. He was serious
and so was I and so I wouldn't go
when he wanted to see me when
he was dying of leukemia. Am I
sorry? Not really. The fear had
gone too deep. The last time I
saw him was in the City Center lobby
and he was jolly—if he just
stared at you and the tears began

it was time to cut and run—
and the cancer had made him lose
a lot of weight and he looked
young and handsome as the night
we picked each other up
in Pop Tunick's long-gone gay bar.
Bill never let me forget that
on the jukebox I kept playing
Lena Horne's "Mad about the Boy."
Why the nagging teasing? It's
a great performance but he
thought it was East Fifties queen
taste. Funny—or, funnily enough—
in dreams, and I dream about him
a lot, he's always the nice guy
I first knew and loved, not
the figure of terror he became.
Oh well. Bill had his hour: he
was a hero, a major in the
Abraham Lincoln Brigade. A dark
Finn who looked not unlike
a butch version of Valentino.
Watch out for Finns. They're
murder when they drink) used
to ride the ferries all the
time, doing the bars along
the waterfront: did you know
that Hoboken has—or had—
more bars to the square inch
(Death. At least twice when

someone I knew and hated
died I felt the joy of vengeance:
I mean I smiled and laughed out
loud: a hateful feeling.
It passes.) to the square inch
than any other city? "Trivia,
Goddess . . ." Through dinner
I wanted to talk more than we
did about Frank's poems. All it
came down to was "experiment
more," "try collages," and "write
some skinny poems" but I like
where he's heading now and
Creative Writing has never
been my trip although I understand
the fun of teaching someone
something fun to do although most people
simply have not got the gift
and where's the point? What
puzzles me is what my friends
find to say. Oh forget it. Reading,
writing, knowing other poets
will do it, if there is
anything doing. The reams
of shit I've read. It would
have been so nice after dinner
to take a ferry boat with Frank
across the Hudson (or West River,
if you prefer). To be on
the water in the dark and

the wonder of electricity—
the real beauty of Manhattan.
Oh well. When they tore down
the Singer Building,
and when I saw the Bogardus building
rusty and coming unstitched in
a battlefield of rubble I deliberately
withdrew my emotional investments
in loving old New York. Except
you can't. I really like
dining out and last night was
especially fine. A full moon
when we parted hung over
Frank and me. Why is this poem
so long? And full of death?
Frank and Doug are young and
beautiful and have nothing
to do with that. Why is this poem
so long? "Enough is as good
as a feast" and I'm a Herrick fan.
I'd like to take that plunge
into Central Park, only I'm
waiting for Darragh Park to phone.
Oh. Doug and Frank. One is light,
the other dark.
Doug is the tall one.

THE
PAYNE
WHITNEY
POEMS

Trip

Wigging in, wigging out:
when I stop to think
the wires in my head
cross: kaboom. How
many trips
by ambulance (five,
count them five),
claustrated, pill addiction,
in and out of mental
hospitals,
the suicidalness (once
I almost made it)
but—I go on?
Tell you all of it?
I can't. When I think
of that, that at
only fifty-one I,
Jim the Jerk, am
still alive and breathing
deeply, that I think
is a miracle.

We Walk

in the garden. Sun
on the river
flashing past. I
dig ivy leaves.
We walk in a
maze. Sun, shine
on. Now it is
one hour later.
Out the window no
sun. Cloud
turbulence and
the wind whistles.
Curious.

Arches

of buildings, this building,
frame a stream of windows
framed in white brick. This
building is fireproof; or else
it isn't: the furnishings first
to go: no, the patients. Patients
on Sundays walk in a small garden.
Today some go out on a group
pass. To stroll the streets and shop.
So what else is new? The sky
slowly/swiftly went blue to gray.
A gray in which some smoke stands.

Linen

Is this the moment?
No, not yet.
When is the moment?
Perhaps there is none.
Need I persist?

This morning I
changed bedding.
At lunch I watched
someone shake out
the cloth, fold and
stow it in a side-
board. Then, the
cigarette moment.
Now, this moment
flows out of me
down the pen and
writes.

I'm glad I have
fresh linen.

Heather and Calendulas

A violet hush: and sunbursts.
An aluminum measure
full of water. Scentlessness.
"Go to church next week?"
Fortuitous as nuts too
salty. Accordion pleats.
The phone bill is buff.
Three postcards of three
paintings. A good review.
Pale green walls and
a white ceiling. Lamps
lit in daylight. Ice.
The temperature 16. In
February. "Laugh and
the world laughs with you."
Die, and you die alone.

Back

from the Frick. The weather
cruel as Henry Clay himself.
Who put that collection together?
Duveen? I forget. It was nice
to see the masterpieces again,
covered with the strikers' blood.
What's with art anyway, that
we give it such precedence?
I love the paintings, that's for sure.
What I really loved today
was New York, its streets and
men selling flowers and hot dogs
in them. Mysterious town houses,
the gritty wind. I used to live
around here but it's changed some.
Why? That was only thirty years ago.

Blizzard

Tearing and tearing
ripped-up bits of paper,
no, it's not paper
it's snow. Blown side-
ways in the wind,
coming in my window
wetting stacked books.
"Mr Park called. He
can't come visiting
today." Of course not,
in this driving icy
weather. How I wish
I were out in it! A
figure like an ex-
clamation point seen
through driving snow.

February 13, 1975

Tomorrow is St. Valentine's:
tomorrow I'll think about
that. Always nervous, even
after a good sleep I'd like
to climb back into. The sun
shines on yesterday's new-
fallen snow and yestereven
it turned the world to pink
and rose and steel-blue
buildings. Helene is restless:
leaving soon. And what then
will I do with myself? Some-
one is watching morning
TV. I'm not reduced to that
yet. I wish one could press
snowflakes in a book like flowers.

Sleep

The friends who come to see you
and the friends who don't.
The weather in the window.
A pierced ear.
The mounting tension and the spasm.
A paper-lace doily on a small plate.
Tangerines.
A day in February: heart-
shaped cookies on St. Valentine's.
Like Christopher, a discarded saint.
A tough woman with black hair.
"I got to set my wig straight."
A gold and silver day begins to wane.
A crescent moon.
Ice on the window.
Give my love to, oh, anybody.

Pastime

I pick up a loaded pen and twiddle it.
After the blizzard
cold days of shrinking snow.
At visiting hours the cars
below my window form up
in a traffic jam. A fast-
moving man is in charge,
herding the big machines
like cattle. Weirdly, it all
keeps moving somehow. I read
a dumb detective story. I
clip my nails: they are as hard
as iron or glass. The clippers
keep sliding off them. Today
I'm shaky. A shave, a bath.
Chat. The morning paper.
Sitting. Staring. Thinking blankly.
TV. A desert kind of life.

What

What's in those pills?
After lunch and I can
hardly keep my eyes
open. Oh, for someone to
talk small talk with.
Even a dog would do.

Why are they hammering
iron outside? And what
is that generator whose
fierce hum comes in
the window? What is a
poem, anyway.

The daffodils, the heather
and the freesias all
speak to me. I speak
back, like St. Francis
and the wolf of Gubbio.

THE
MORNING
OF THE
POEM

The Morning of the Poem

July 8 or July 9 the eighth surely, certainly
      1976 that I know
Awakening in western New York blurred barely
      morning sopping dawn
Globules face to my face, a beautiful face, not
      mine: Baudelaire's skull:
Force, fate, will, and, you being you: a
      painter, you drink
Your Ovaltine and climb to the city roof, "to
      find a view," and
I being whoever I am get out of bed holding
      my cock and go to piss
Then to the kitchen to make coffee and toast
      with jam and see out
The window two blue jays ripping something white
      while from my mother's
Room the radio purls: it plays all night she leaves
      it on to hear
The midnight news then sleeps and dozes
      until day which now it is,
Wakening today in green more gray, why did
      your lithe blondness
In Remsen handsomeness mix in my mind with
      Baudelaire's skull? which
Stands for strength and fierceness, the dedication
      of the artist?

How easily I could be in love with you,
       who do not like to be touched,
And yet I do not want to be in love with you,
       nor you with me,
"Strange business" the chinky Chinaman said and
       from the kitchen window
The jays are fatter than any jays I ever saw
       before and hanging
In a parlor floor in far-off Chelsea I'm
       glad there is a
Watercolor of me in blue shorts, sitting
       beside a black Britannica
And a green-glass-shaded student lamp and
       a glass of deep red wine
Ruby wine the throat of a hummingbird
       hanging on speeding
Wings in fierce blue delphinium depths I think
About those two blue jays, like me, too
       chubby, and Baudelaire's skull,
That sees in the tattered morning the passing of
The lost and indigent, the lost, the way
       the day when I arose
Seemed lost and trash-picking for a meatless morsel,
       a stinking
Bone, such as in this green unlovely village
       one need never
Seek or fear and you descend to your studio
       leaving on your roof
The exhalation of Baudelaire's image of
       terror which is

Not terror but the artist's (your) determination
        to be strong
To see things as they are too fierce and yet
        not too much: in
Western New York, why Baudelaire? In Chelsea,
        why not? Smile,
July day. Why did Baudelaire wander in? Don't
        I love Heine more? Or
Walt Whitman, Walt? No, they come to my death-
        bed and one by one take my hand
And say, "So long, old man," and who was it
        who in the Café Montana told,
In all seriousness, that the triumph of Mrs S.,
        future Duchess of W., was that
"They say she's a circus in bed." I like to
        dwell on that, the caged lions
And the whips, ball-balancing seals, "And now,
        without a net . . ." the odious
Clowns: boring Ensor and pseudo-symbolism of
        something meaning something
That doesn't mean a thing at all: the simplicity
        of true drama, a trained and
Modulated voice, a hand that rises of itself:
        "La commedia non par finita;
Ma pure è finita" pleasant to be
        Goldoni and meet Mr Tiepolo in
The square, or Longhi, Guardi, or am I mixing
        up my dates: somebody was older
Than somebody and Goldoni went off to France
        on another gray morning in

Which the firs crowd too thickly on these village
        lawns: Chestnut Hill Road,
But the blight came and there are no chestnuts;
        the blight came, and there
Are no elms; only spruce and maples, maple saplings
        springing up in hedges,
A skinny weed, and this weed, this wild yellow
        flower lower and larger than
A buttercup, not lacquer yellow, more the yellow
        of a marsh marigold, meaty
Like it, though not so large, not nearly so
        large, sprinkled in the weedy
Wild-flower lawn, for God's sake, what is your
        name? "Will you have the watermelon
And the iced coffee, dear?" "Comrades, leave me
        read my *Times*." She sets
The dishes out just so, as though to please me
        and to please her, a right
Way to do things and that is how she does them. The watermelon
        is fresh
And good and behind this grunt of words I see
        you, Baudelaire's mask your sign,
Legs apart, addressed to your easel, squeezing
        out the tubes of oils
Whose names you know: what is that green you
        use so much of, that seems to
Devour itself? Nor can I quite forget what someone
        said: "I got her number:
'Why did you tell him homosexuality is a neurosis?' "
        I said, "She said

She didn't say it, but she did." Hard to
        achieve with so much information
Available, so little to be believed. Last July
        was an inferno, tempests of
Rain, then seared grass, this July overcast
        with hottish afternoons: I
Begrudge that far-off island in Penobscot Bay,
        mossy walks and Twin Flower
Corner, icy swims in early morning off pebble
        beaches, the smell of juniper
Where my dead best friend will always walk
        beside me, stride ahead of me.
"When I walk with you, all I see is the heels
        of your sneakers": were
You buried in your sneakers? Of course not,
        though in a tender joke you were:
A nosegay tossed on the coffin: but this is not
        your poem, your poem I may
Never write, too much, though it is there and
        needs only to be written down
And one day will and if it isn't it doesn't matter:
        the truth, the absolute
Of feeling, of knowing what you know, that is
        the poem, like
The house for sale buried in a luxuriance of
        overgrown foundation planting
Across the street upon this hill (Taxus,
        Cotoneaster), the doctor has more
Patients in Buffalo: he moved there: I'd rather
        stay here and starve, well,

Sort of starve: yesterday I tripped on a scatter
        rug and slam fell full length,
The wind knocked out of me: "Shall I call a
        doctor?" "Please don't talk"
"Are you hurt? Can I help you?" "Shut the fuck
        up" I thought I'd smashed
My kneecap—you know, like when you really
        wham your funny bone, only
More so—but I got up and felt its nothing-
        broken-tenderness and
Hobbled down this everlasting hill to distant
        Bell's and bought
Edible necessities: small icy cans of concentrated
        juice, lemon, lime, orange,
Vast puffy bags of bread, Smucker's raspberry jam,
        oatmeal, but not the good,
The Irish kind (travel note: in New York City you
        almost cannot buy a bowl
Of oatmeal: I know, I've tried: why bother: it
        would only taste like paste)
and hobbled home, studying the for-sale house
        hidden in scaly leaves
The way the brownstone facing of your house is
        coming off in giant flakes: there's
A word for that sickness of the stone but I
        can't remember it (you'll find
It in that fascinating book *Brick and Brownstone*:
        illustrative photograph)
And in July you take a picture in progress out,
        your street in snow,

Air conditioners capped with snow and in the
       distance the problem,
An office building straight from Babylon: a
       friend said of you, "With people,
he's awfully good," meaning, I surmise, "kind,
       considerate," "Oh," I said,
"When he has to, he can put his foot down," "I'm
       very glad," our friend
Said, "to hear *that*." Not that he or I meant
       you have a taint
Of toughness, just, well, time passes and
       sometimes you must say "No"
Or, "Don't tread on me" but don't change, I
       like you as you are, laughing
So loud in Sagaponack the summer neighbors
       sent the maid to poke through
Privet and say "There's too much noise": we were
       stunned: complaints about
Laughing? We go on, but, of course, it's not
       quite the same under
An almost autumn sky, a swimming pool awash
       with cinnamon and gentian
(The sky's the swimming pool, that is) why is
       each day dawning so alike? Overcast,
Or gray: choose one: and then there was the just-
       before-morning electric storm
Night before last: two killed by bolt in a
       Batavia park: my room lighting up
Bright enough to read by. "Fear no more the heat
       of the sun, nor the all-

Dreaded thunder-stone," funny, lightning doesn't
        scare me any more, it thrills,
So long as I'm indoors, in bed by preference,
        with pillows under which to tuck
My head against the louder claps. I'm very brave.
        Then a shovelful of earth
Is thrown into the open grave and rattles on
        the coffin. Oh goodbye, goodbye.
I want to go away into that blue or dark or
        certain or uncertain land: why
Can't we know that it is there and there we'll
        meet and grow in friendship
As we have here? You know that Austrian operetta,
        don't you, *The Land of Smiles?*
That is not what I mean. I'm often happiest
        walking crosstown on a bright
And icy day when up above mare's-tails sparkle and
        I stop to inspect the junk
In junk-shop windows and pass on feasting my eyes
        on what to me is beefy
Handsomeness, sexiness, I don't want it really,
        just to recollect or think,
My, that's nice, warm flesh on a cold, cold
        day: today, July, country edge,
There's almost a chill, and the knee I fell on
        throbs more than
Yesterday. What a drag. Michael Lally is a fine
        poet and looks straight
Into your eyes. I know someone else who looks
        deep into your eyes and under

The curly hair the lies are manufactured. Mostly,
        it delights me, like
A farce, the need to dramatize, to make out, "Oh
        I was beautiful, oh the most
Famous men all fell for me and slipped it up
        my cooze. I've seen
'em all!" I believe you, dear. More kinds of
        conifers than spruce grow
On this hill. I wish I knew their names, I have
        a friend, a botanist,
Who could tell them to me, one by one. He lives
        in London Terrace and this
Is the London Terrace story. There's something
        called the Poison Line:
When someone, children mostly, goes, say, munching
        in the woods and gets sick
The doctors set the phone wires flashing to
        hospitals, horticultural
Gardens, informed New York. It was 3 a.m., my
        friend was asleep in
London Terrace. The phone. Off in Virginia a young
        man had quarreled
With his family so he went out in the yard and
        gathered castor beans.
They have a hard shell and if you swallow them
        like that they pass
Harmlessly through. He crushed them first. Eight
        is a lethal dose. He
Picked ten. A young man in Virginia. "What happened?"
        "I said, induce

Vomiting. I'm sure it was too late." "Did he die?"
   "I don't know: I
Tried to check back but I couldn't make contact."
   And all that castor
Oil they used to pour down me when I was a kid.
   Pity the young Virginian.
And still it's chill and overcast and in the afternoon
   we went next door
To tea: a house I'd lived next door to for
   forty years and never been inside
Of, not once, before. Mrs Blank, the dead, the former
   owner, wasn't much for
Entertaining high-school boys. She died mad, her
   little hands clenched in
Monkey fists and wouldn't eat her food. Her husband,
   the arborist, he's
Gone too, and handsome Larry, crushed by a car
   against the back wall of a garage:
Die, die, die, and only pray the pain won't be more
   than you can bear. But
What you must bear, you will. I've known a
   murderer (or two): or were
They only bragging? Not everyone is quite so nice
   as my gentle Grandma Ella
Sleeping away off there in Albert Lea, Minnesota,
   where even the lake
Is named Lake Albert Lea: who was he? A surveyor,
   it seems to me: you can
See the lake in this snapshot of my mother, kneeling
   on the lawn, using

Her turned-over hat to hold a big bunch of sweet
          William: stop stirring
The rice and come with me to Maine and we'll settle
          once for all which
Is woundwort and which Jill-over-the-ground: but
          you're painting, or sketching
In big charcoal strokes what will become a painting:
          I'm posing, seated
By the tall window and the Ming tree, and look
          out across the Chelsea street
And up to where a handsome muscular man in just
          a towel leans out into
The snow (it isn't always July, you know) to see
          what's going on: my heart
Goes pitta-pat, but you, you won't even down
          your brush and take a peek:
I call that dedication: painting, stirring rice,
          scooting off
To see the great Arletty as Garance: busy, busy:
          happy, happy? Sometimes
I think so, surely hope so: perhaps what I mean
          is happier, happier,
Plunged in work, sorting out your head: "Bonjour,
          madame, I am little
Marcel Proust" "I take the subway, then the cross-
          town bus, the small Rembrandt
On the wall," that's rather grand you know, however
          small, and to the collection
Now is added one by you and that too is pleasing
          and not ungrand: July

Days pass, the brushes slide and pull the paint:
      out your window
Do the roses bloom? I hope so: how I love roses!
      Bunches of roses on
The dining table, Georg Arends, big and silver-
      pink with sharply
Bent-back petals so the petals make a point: no
      other rose does that:
or Variegata di Bologna, streaked and freaked
      in raspberries and cream,
A few gathered into an amethyst wineglass:
      nothing like it and I
Love them, not over yet early in July, this cold
      July, the grass for once
Is not overmown, burnt off: the mower is set too
      close, it frustrates
Me. Typing in my undershorts, I'm cold; abroad,
      England, France,
Denmark, Germany (oh yes, and Italy), they've had
      a four-week heat wave and
A drought. The pastures for the cows are all
      burnt off, only the grapes
In France are happy, what a bonanza there will
      be, wine, rich and grapy,
No treat, alas, for those who don't imbibe: rich
      as those Poiret robes
And dresses I went to see in the cellar of the
      Fashion Institute of Technology:
A brown that isn't purple, gamboge, celadon lined
      with jade, fat fur cuffs,

Turbans stuck with black aigrettes, luxury and
        wit: tell me, you who know,
What is that bird big as a duck that's not a
        duck on the grass with a black
Bib and dark tan stripes, is it a kind of dove
        or pigeon? What would I gain
By knowing? Like West 20th Street, West 22nd
        Street, a white high rise at
Number 360 where the International Supermarket
        nestles? And the Seminary
Enclosing a court of grass and trees, dark-
        green-smelling cut-out shapes on
The evening we took our stroll there. Nearby,
        the sadomasochistic bars
With men in nails and boots and leather and
        the heavier sort of denim,
Clanking keys, the risky docks: you'd be
        well advised to keep
Away from there: a lot of it of course is
        just for show (children playing
Dress-ups) but some of it is more, how you say,
        for real: I saw a man's
Back where someone had played ticktacktoe
        with a knife. His wife has
Left him. "Have some speed: makes you feel
        real sexy," get away from me you
Poet with no talent, only a gift to destroy:
        when our best poet was invited
To review one of your little offerings I said,
        "Won't it be like

Reviewing your reflection in an oil slick?"
So many lousy poets
So few good ones
What's the problem?
No innate love of
Words, no sense of
How the thing said
Is in the words, how
The words are themselves
The thing said: love,
Mistake, promise, auto
Crack-up, color, petal,
The color in the petal
Is merely light
And that's refraction:
A word, that's the poem.
A blackish-red nasturtium.
Roses shed on
A kitchen floor, a
Cool and scented bed
To loll and roll on.
I wish I had a rose
Or butterfly tattoo:
But where? Here on
My arm or my inner
Thigh, small, where
Only the happy few
Might see it? I'll
Never forget that
Moving man, naked to

The waist a prize
Fight buckle on his
Belt (Panama) and
Flying high on each
Pectoral a bluebird
On tan sky skin. I
Wanted to eat him up:
No such luck. East
28th Street, 1950.
How the roses pass.
I wish I were posing on West 22nd Street, seated
      by a window and the plants,
While your brush makes whorls in your painty
      palette and I watch
The street and kids skim on skateboards: it's
      summer, it's July,
Or else it's winter, December, January, February
      and the kids are gloved and
Bundled up and it's snowball-fighting time: "Gonna
      rub your face in it!" and
Does and one breaks loose and runs crying home.
      In the highest window of
A house across the street a German shepherd rests
      his paws on the sill and
Hangs his head out, gazing down, gazing down,
      gazing down and taking in the scene:
These flaming Christmas plants bring to mind
      Joel Poinsett: must read up on
Him: and in September (it isn't winter, it's
      summer, it's July) I'll see your

New crop of work: I'll like that: are you staying
  off the sauce? Remember what
The doctor said: I am: remembering and staying
  off: mostly it's not
So hard (indeed): did you know a side effect of
  Antabuse can be to make
You impotent? Not that I need much help in that
  department these days: funny,
I remember walking under the palms on liberty in
  1943 with a soldier
I had just picked up and in my sailor suit some-
  thing long and stony as the
Washington Monument I wanted to hide from the
  officer coming toward me: I
Guess I was afraid he'd see it, get the picture
  of what was about to and in fact
Did happen, and send me back to base. Key West!
  the beautiful white houses
With the louvered upstairs, downstairs porches,
  the heavy oaks densely hung
With Spanish moss, the tall blue-blacks with
  hauteur and disdain, beyond
The chain fence, in their eyes and carriage:
  "Stay out of Jungle Town" "You
Bet I will": the barracuda and the angelfish,
  stars like the Koh-i-noor
And a full moon reflecting back the star-encrusted
  sea, a face-
Enveloping moon I want to see again casting
  black velvet shadows of

The palms and broad banana leaves. But that son
      of a bitch, that soldier:
He was trade. I was much too young in those days
      for that jazz and walked
Away and left him to bring himself off anyway
      he chose, by fist, I suppose.
Sitting typing in my underwear on this chilly
      soggy morning while the rain
Comes and goes: I'd like to live in T-shirt
      and undershorts,
Bare feet, my Danish silver chain, a gift from
      the one who mattered most,
Gone as last year's roses (Souvenir de la
      Malmaison): that I'll never again
Fall asleep with my head on his chest or shoulder
      that kind of bugs me and
Pictures linger clearly: outside the Hotel Chelsea
      he stood across
The street, in tweed, a snappy dresser, feet
      apart, head turned
In an Irish profile, holding an English attaché
      case, looking for
A cab to Madison Avenue, late, as usual, looking
      right out of a bandbox,
As usual. I won't make a catalogue of all the
      times we were together I
Remember: just one more: slim and muscular you
      come out of the shower,
Wrap a towel around your waist and lean on the
      washbasin with one

Hand, then squirting Noxzema shaving foam to
      smear on your
Sharp-boned face and shave. Wilkinson Injector.
      Green eyes in the
Medicine-chest mirror. You said, "I'm sorry:
      everything just got too
Fucked up. Thank you for the book." That's
      what I get. Was it worth it?
On the whole, I think it was. Toot-toot-
      tootsie, goodbye.
The low and seamless cloud is over us, the
      all there is to it
Morning sky: again: day after day but today
      is breakthrough day, the sun
Burns through then goes away then returns
      more brightly, a breezy coolness
At the window and at my back stirs the
      Peperomia, the grass here and across
The street (HOUSE FOR SALE) almost glares: a
      lawnmower makes its heavy hum
Advancing and retreating in a dance, a reel,
      sweet Jesus, it's my nephew
Mike mowing his granny's lawn. "Mike, come in
      and have a Coke" "I
Will, Uncle Jim, soon as I'm done," he wears an
      Ace bandage on an elbow where
He cracked it canoeing at scout camp last week.
      He likes to
Ski, he likes to wrestle, he has a ten-speed
      bike, he likes to shoot small

Game in the fields and woods behind their house
      on the other side of town
Where you get the best views of the sunsets,
      violet laced with orange and
White fritters: kimono colors: oh, I saw those
      jays again at dawn
Tearing at something white and the something white
      was a white petunia, the jays
Are real workers at their job and the petunia row
      is shredded almost
All away: tall and sentinel above what's left
      of them a dense row of lilies
Long in bud, soon to bloom with their foxy
      adolescent girl smell: repellent
Yet sexy and crotch-calling: Baudelaire, I'd like
      to share a pipe with
You (we could both wear gloves, for fear of
      the itch) and I would be a nineteenth-
Century dandy dude smelling strongly of vanilla
      bean: did you know that
Vanilla is an orchid? And so are you, my cutie,
      reeking of poppers
In the parlor car, Southampton bound: you must have
      had quite a night of it
At the sauna: tell me what you did: you did? Oh wow.
      "Jimmy," you said, "don't tell
Anyone you have syphilis," "Of course I'm going to
      tell X, I have no secrets
From him; anyway, I've already told Y and Z, they
      didn't take it big and

Laughed when I said they should have blood tests."
      I told
X in a skylit room and he was, to my surprise, cross,
      unsympathetic, in fact
Disgusted: it was all out of his range, the range of
Things that happen to folks you know: "You must
      be more careful
About catching syphilis," "When you had your accident
      I didn't say be
More careful of getting hit by trains," and "If
      I'm to have any sex
At all to do so I must run a risk" (back in the
      Turkish-bath days): no
One stayed mad, I got well, and when I went to my
      doctor for my last
Injection I walked in on his wake. Within a week
      his aide had killed
Himself, his wife had burned to death in her living
      room, all on morphine
And my doctor had cared, had tried to care for
      them all, others too.
In the cool insistent sun of this changed day—
      Scotland has gone away, western
New York is, it seems, back to stay—beneath the north
      window I see out of when I
Look left, large-leaved Solomon's-seal make light
      and shadows on themselves
Moved by air, the air is like the gray-haired striding
      slim-waisted

Man who went through the automatic doors yesterday
        afternoon at the store ahead
Of me: I wanted to tap his shoulder and say, "Excuse
        me, I'm sure that we have
Met: were you in the class of '41?" Instead I grabbed
        a cart, went wheeling
up and down the aisles trying to get a front view of
        him and see how he was
Hung and what his face was like. But when I reached
        my goal he was wearing
(I surmise) Jockey shorts (I curse the inventor of
        Jockey shorts) and his face
Was weathered like someone who plays golf a lot,
        not handsome but a kind of
Face I like: he was smelling and squeezing honeydews
        (I'll be your honeydew,
Your Persian melon) when suddenly he raised
        his head and passed
Me, as on a tray, a plain and questioning
        straightforward hostile look: I
Dropped a green bell pepper (10¢) in the cart and
        went wheeling on:
"What am I forgetting?": when I was young I didn't go
        for guys my age, I sought
Out men his age (fifty-five?) about the age I am
        now, but now men my age are not
Interested in me, they seek out beauties, blue-eyed,
        blond and tanned, or in other
Colorations, the cult of youth, I'd like to kick them
        all: there's no democracy:

"Time to retire" when I saw a broad-beamed lady
          also frown and give me a
Different kind of look: "I know your face . . . aren't
          you . . ." you're
Right, dear, you sat in front of me in senior English
          or was it chemistry
Or French or study hall? I grab a ton of milk and
          head for the express check-
Out lane, first shoving the unwanted bell pepper
          in among some
Dog food. The man had vanished. What a great love
          ours might have been, doing
It on the golf course at 2 a.m. (he was clearly
          married, all the good ones
Are). At the hardware store I bought an onion
          chopper, glass and shrill orange
Plastic, and an old-fashioned mousetrap, up-dated
          with a scented, simulated
Piece of wooden cheese. I hate mousetraps: waking
          in the night to hear
The thrashing crashing struggle on the kitchen
          floor, the hideous trapped
Scream of pain: and I'm the one who will have
          to deal with it: drowning? an
Elephant gun? Besides, what's wrong with mice? A
          few mouse turds
Are soon swept up. Now rats, rats are another story.
          This day, I want to
Send it to you, the sound of stirring air, soft
          sunlight, quivering trees

That shake their needles and leaves like fingers
          improvising on a keyboard
Scriabin in his softest mood, and the wind
          rises and it all goes Delius,
The sky pale and freshly washed, the blue flaked
          off here and there and
Showing white, flat and skimpy clouds haunting
          a bright green, a soft blue day.
I'm sorry the full moon is past, still, there
          are shadows on the grass
Fit to lie in; study the leaves or blades and let
          the scurrying
Black ants traverse your arm, your hand: the dog
          next door got in the trash
Again: a black and husky chummy fellow, him I
          can't get mad at. The days
Go by, soon I will go back, back to Chelsea, my
          room that faces south
And the ailanthus tree wound with ivy, my records,
          stacks and stacks of them,
Spohr's Double Quartet, Ida Cox, and sit in your
          parlor on the squishy chairs
On West 22nd Street, the Fauré Second Piano quartet,
          mirrors and pictures
On the walls: next weekend I hear you're going
          To Sagaponack for a double
Birthday party and half of it is you: 37 meets
          49: many happy returns to
You and You and years and years to come: today
          is a year, a morning, this

Morning was a year, I got up at six? six-thirty?
        on the grass there lay one
Streak of morning light: the days and their different
        lights: when I
Was a child in Washington they took me to the
        theater to see Edward
Everett Horton in *Springtime for Henry* (in which
        that master of the double
Take toured for years: catch him with Helen Broderick
        and Fred and Ginger
And Eric Blore in *Top Hat*) and when the curtain
        went up on the second
Act my breath caught: it was the light: I'd seen
        that light before in Chevy
Chase: an empty living room
        with chintz:
An old theatrical effect: then someone entered:
        left, right, center? Who
Cares? It wasn't the play I liked—too young to
        know what it was
All about—it was the magic of the rising
        of the curtain and the slanting
In of dusty golden autumn light. And earlier,
        before the divorce, at Virginia
Gold's family farm in stony Virginia, I went
        paddling bare-ass in a
Brook with another little boy: when I got back
        my mother raised heck:
"I told you *not* to go in that brook" "I didn't
        go in the brook" (how

Did they always know? I thought I was such an
        accomplished liar: I
Became a pretty good one later) "Then why are
        your B.V.D.s on
Inside out?" Unanswerable questions. The big
        barn had been struck by
Lightning and burned down. The men were rebuilding
        it: Mrs Gold fed the
Chickens and let me help: the pigs were big and
        to be kept away from: they
were mean: on the back porch was the separator,
        milk and cream, luxurious
Ice cream, the best, the very best, and on the
        front porch stood a spinet
Whose ivory keys had turned pale pink: why? There
        was only one
Book on the parlor table and it was Lindbergh's
        We: how can I know that?
I couldn't read: someone told me no doubt and
        no doubt it was Virginia
Gold, she was a schoolteacher, I'm pretty sure.
        I don't remember much about
Her except her blueberry muffins and later
        she and my mother had
A terrible quarrel on the telephone—the
        harsh and hateful voices made me
Sick—and never met again. Mr Gold drove us
        in a Model T or
Touring car to catch a train and in the Union
        Station my father, Mark, was waiting

For us: heavy, jolly, well-read man, you've
        been gone a long time—
More than thirty years—and time I suppose
        has swept all the Golds
Under the carpet too. But I forgot: one of
        the best days at the farm:
The women put their bonnets on and I went
        with them up a hot dusty road
To fields with rock outcrops (watch out for
        snakes) and gathered poke-
Weed. Fried ham and pokeweed, and, in New
        Brunswick, a side order of
Fiddlehead ferns. Europe bores me: it's too
        late: I mean I'm too late:
I've been there: no, it isn't that: I love
        architecture more than anything,
Bernini and Palladio and Laurana, a certain
        church in Venice, Mauro
Coducci, Buonarroti's windows on the Farnese
        Palace. Architecture?
What about Donatello and della Quercia,
        Canova and Verrocchio, the Pisani?
Music and dancing, acting: the Grand Canal in
        autumn after a week of rain:
The water pours from mountains and turns milky-
        green, the tourists
And the vapid rich leave and you are left with
        infinite riches,
The Istrian stone with the silver-pink cast to
        it of Georg Arends that

After a rainstorm enflames itself: no: that's
       the bricks (Istrian
Stone and bricks contrasted) that become petals
       of roses, blossoming
Stone. Black gondolas glide by, the sure-footed
       gondoliers bending and
Leaning on their poles, wearing green velvet
       slippers. On Diaghilev's
Tomb a French count left his calling
       card: more suitable
Than withering flowers. I left only a glance
       and a thought.
But Europe—split, twisted, shivering-leaved
       olive trees,
Grapevines strung high in swags between
       poplar trees—Europe isn't
Home. The rolling farmland of New York, or better still
       Maine and its coast and
Bays and islands, New Brunswick, Nova Scotia,
       white clapboard
Houses with red geraniums inside sparkling
       windows, eating lobster, greedily,
Vermont with a New Year gift of hellish cold and
       deep, glittering, blinding
Snow: lie face down in it and die: please don't
       die, get up and go inside
Where the logs snap and crackle and smoke and
       give off their
Heart- and flesh-warming smell: the beautiful
       humorous white whippet

No longer lies, legs in the air, on the green
        velvet Victorian couch under
Mrs Appleyard's painting on velvet of an epergne
        full of fruit: can't one,
Just one, mortal person or animal be immortal,
        live
Forever? Not shriveling like Tithonus, not in
        an improbable Cloud-Cuckoo-
Land you'd like to but can't quite believe in:
        ageless, immortal, speedy
here in Vermont, chasing rabbits, having a wonderful
        roll in the horse shit:
"Yum! Good!" "Whippoorwill! *What* have you done?"
        (His Master's Voice), the
Graceful tail curling down and in between his
        legs: can a tail curl down
Shamefacedly? His could, and he could strew
        a house with trash, leave
An uninviting mess on stairs: "Surprise! Surprise!"
        or the night I came in
And found between me and my bed the contents
        of a three-pound box
Of the choicest candy: a cheval-de-frise of
        liqueur chocolates: and,
Most beautiful of all, on a long long lawn running,
        racing as whippets
Are bred to do and leaping straight into
        Kenward's arms, who
Casually closed them: quite an act! (That moment in

Serenade when the dancer soars across the stage,
        turns, legs in extension,
Full in the male dancer's face and he
        clasps her
By the waist. They freeze. Patricia. Nicky.)
        Yes, that whippet is
The one I nominate for terrestrial immortality:
        "They say that when
The moon is dark a thin white dog goes racing up
        and down Apple Hill,
You see the white scuts of deer fly off to hide,
        the skunks
Scuttle under maidenhair, a pond reflects the night
        and—this is the scary part—
Out of the 'transpicuous gloom' a dog
        named Nightingale
Materializes. I wouldn't live there if you
        paid me." Love, love
Is immortal. Whippoorwill, I know that.
How can I know that? God knows, I may be dumb:
        may be! Was the grave
Lined with moss, a handful of wild flowers tossed
        in, did marl rattle
On a pine box? Or were the ashes scattered
        where milkweed floss
Carry their seeds like little men?
        I see a man
        naked and handsome
        in the pond. I
        see a horse

lumber up a hill.
I see tomatoes
set to ripen on
a sill. I see
a dog, two dogs:
Whippoorwill, of
the mysterious
determined inner life:
"Let me in, let
me out, let me wind
myself in a
crazy quilt," and
pretty, trembling,
hysterical Rossignol
leaping out of
the back seat of
an open car never
to be seen again.
Rest, lie at rest
among these hills
and mountains
in autumn flowing
in maple colors:
crimson, yellow,
orange, green
freaked with white:
ripeness, a resurrection,
leaves, leaves, leaves,
when it's time,
cover us all.

•

Another day, another dolor. A shopping list:
    watermelon wedge
    blueberries (2 boxes)
                  (In a far recess of summer
                  Monks are playing soccer)
    Bread (Arnold sandwich)
    Yogurt (plain)
    Taster's Choice
    Brim
    Milk (2 qts)
    Whipping cream
    Dispoz-A-Lite
    Lee Riders
    Something for Sunday dinner
    Blue Top-Siders (10½)
    Little apples
    Paper napkins?
    Guerlain Impériale
    Steak
    Noxzema medicated shave foam
    Alka-Seltzer
    Baume Bengué
    K-Y
There is not one store in this good-sized village
    that will deliver. Guess
I'll have to call a cab: while I ate my oatmeal
    and read the *Courier Express*

(that fireman who's been doing it with adolescent
      girls got twenty-five years:
"Sodomy in the first degree; sodomy in the second
      degree: sodomy in the third
Degree": what's that all about? and a theater group
      is putting on a show called
Bullets in the Potato Salad) it began heartily
      to rain: not in drops,
In liquid shafts driving into the lawn and earth
      drilling holes, beating up
The impatiens, petunias, lilies (whose cock-like
      buds are turning orange) and
The bluey-purple flowers like larkspur only not
      so nice (there is a bowl
Of everlasting on my dressing table: I'd like to
      dump it out: I hate the feel
Of their papery stiff petals: why feel it then?
      Can't help myself, feel, feel)
Rain! this morning I liked it more than sun, if I were
      younger I would have
Run out naked in it, my hair full of Prell, chilled
      and loving it, cleansed,
Refreshed, at one with quince and apple trees. As it was
      it was enough to
Sit and eat and watch it, wet weavings of a summer morning,
      and try to stop
My mother from slamming every window and shutting out
      the smell,
The sweet, sweet, sweet smell of morning rain, in
      your nose, on bare skin.

"Don't shut that window: it isn't coming in." "Well,
        it *might* come in and
I'm the one who will have to clean it up." Slam. I
        open it again: "This
Rain will last about thirty seconds (it did), I'm watching
        it and if
It starts to blow in I'll close the window." "See
        you do: and you can
Mop it." I read about Brian Goodell the great
        Olympic teen-
Age swimmer and feel like smashing dishes (never
        forget the morning when
Mother yelled, "Don't you *dare* throw that light bulb
        at me!" I didn't: I
Smashed it on the wall: when you're sound asleep
        and someone yanks the
Covers off . . .). Two people obstinate as mules, who
        love each other: I wonder
Though, do I really love anybody? I think I'll can
        it with this love
Stuff for a while; when a friend made a joke
        about death I
Laughed too and said, "I'm ready to go any
        time." "Why, Jimmy!" she said:
"No, I mean it." I wish it was 1938 or '39 again
        and Bernie was sleeping
With me in the tent at the back of the yard
        the time we got up
In the starry night and went downhill,
        down Olean Road, downhill again

And through the pasture where the cows coughed
      and exhaled warm breath,
Barefoot among the cow flops (Dutchman's
      razors) and stands of thistles and
Buttercups the cows won't eat (if you're not
      a farm boy, coming up against
A cow the size of a battleship is not unnerving) (now what
      was the name of that boy, the cowfucker,
Who lived down Olean Road? To each his own), sharp cropped
      dewy grass between toes to where Cazenovia
Creek made a big bend and the warm and muddy water was deep
      enough to swim in. Starlighted silent
Ripples as you stroke: the thick black shapes against the
      black are old big trees: Bernie climbs
Up into one and dives: night air is loudly shattered by a
      splash: the crash when the curtain rises
In *La Traviata* on Act One: Violetta is "having an at home":
      we don't have towels and stand on the clay
Bank to let the air dry us off, grabbing at each other's cocks:
      only, really it's not that kind of friendship:
Mostly because Bernie was Catholic and worried about confession
      and such: me, in those days I was randy most
All the time. The back doorbell rings: it's the laundry
      lad, he's got my slacks, "a buck twenty-five,"
He's funny-faced, skinny and muscular, red-gold hair, and, sigh,
      wears a broad plain wedding ring. I make
Myself sound like a dirty old man, a hound, always on the sniff:
      the truth is I haven't had sex in over a year
And a half: as Ethel sang: *When the only man in the world*
                    You care about

Talks of somebody else
And
Walks
Out ... (Mr Cole Porter, and I
                    May be misquoting)
Bob, who am I kidding? In some ways you were bright and gifted,
        in others, you were one dumb ox. I insist,
Though, you were gifted, much more than, somehow, you could
        let yourself know: spending it in trivial
Ways: no: hiding it under the sod, where you couldn't find
        or use it. Love letters are said to make dull
Reading: I have one from you that's as good as Byron, and on
        it you wrote in your weird hand, "I'm not
Going to read this over because if I do I'll tear it up." I
        keep that letter, but only once have I taken it
Out and read it over: ouch: cologne in a shaving cut. Where
        are you? I don't want to know (yes I do)
How are you? (who cares?) did you and your wife divorce (that,
        I am curious about: splitting after twenty-three
Years?) who got the pretty farmhouse in Jersey where the yellow
        Japanese iris I gave you flourish? and why did
You keep saying no to a clump of big white chrysanthemums? Splendid
        against deep grass at the end of August, almost
Unkillable, a perfect perennial for a lazy gardener, which you
        were (so am I), again, old chum, goodbye: I
Did a better job with Donald, I winkled him out of an antique
        shop and back into life and I didn't know I'd
Done it until he told me: they break your heart and then they
        thank you: your heart! They break your

Balls and they say, "You really helped me: you know, *I*
        was in *love* with you; I think": the first,
The very first, Paul, the one in high school (he is now one
        dead duck), later said, after that winter of
Silent midnight walks in the deep snow, "I couldn't take it:
        it was too heavy: you put on too much
Pressure: but I kept that letter you wrote me in that empty
        freezing house: it touched me." Every time
He thought he'd got out from under I thought of a new trick:
        a dozen dark red roses for his mother (she,
She was nice), "Paul, I'm very fond of Jimmy: I've invited him
        to dinner to help celebrate my birthday," that
Must have pissed him off: I went though and enjoyed myself:
        with Paul's parents, surprisingly, I was
Never shy, bragging about my Schuyler descent and who Alexander
        Hamilton married (it wasn't me): or the dark
Summer night when Bernie—we were getting old, planning to
        go to Guatemala, we still slept in the tent—and
I crept into their darkened house and up the stairs and into Paul's
        room and woke him up: he was furious but got
Dressed and came out to the Roycroft Inn and got mildly drunk
        on gin and squirt: I knew it would work:
Paul was nuts about Bernie. All Bernie ever said about him
        was, "I saw your heartthrob the other night
At Kleinhans Music Hall: I knew him by his piggy little eyes."
        Then one day (snap your fingers, tap your toes)
It was over: I passed him on the street and looked at him unsheepishly
        and said, "Hi, Paul," he was startled into saying
"Hello" for the first time in a year: later, not much later but
        later, comparing notes on our first acquaintance

With queer ("gay," if you prefer) New York, he said, "One night
      I hocked my one good suit so I could go to the
One Two Three Club and hear Roger Stearns play Cole Porter: it's
      cheap if you sit at the bar": "I'm well
Aware: did you get picked up?" "I'm not telling": which meant
      he didn't: he was not good-looking enough to
Make it in that kept-boy crowd (between sets Roger Stearns sat at
      his own table with the most beautiful sailor
I ever saw—on the nights when I went there). We were sitting on
      a sofa, side by side, and Paul reached out and
Put his hand on my crotch and fiddled with my fly (the crust) and
      got the horselaugh of his life. He sure did
Have little piggy eyes. "Let's take a walk to Stinking Pond."
      "O.K.," he said: he was a realist in a
Sickening sort of way. Years afterward he called me at the Museum
      and said, "Let's get together": "I'd love to
But I'm going out of town: a Museum show I'm working on." Finis:
      Paul, with the peculiar cock, short, thick,
Twisted, lumpy, like a piece of rotted rope (give it to the
      oakum pickers), I'll remember you one way,
Sitting in front of me in I wonder which class, with beautiful
      Patricia sitting in front of you and leaning
Back while you slowly combed her hair. You were also Luther
      Smeltzer's pet: that I did not like: it made
Me jealous: Mr Smeltzer, who opened windows for me on flowering
      fields and bays where the water greenly danced,
Knifed into waves by wind: the day he disclosed William Carlos
      Williams to us, writing a short and seemingly
Senseless poem on the blackboard—I've searched the collected
      poems and am never sure which it is (Wallace

Stevens, Marianne Moore, Elizabeth Bishop, I found for myself:
        even then, there's a chance that I was somewhat
Smarter than Luther Smeltzer: "Who, where, when, what and why":
        his journalism lessons were not precisely novel)—
And telling us about a book that based its narrative on Homer,
        "stream of consciousness," Dorothy Richardson,
After class I asked where could I get that book? "Chuckle chuckle:
        when you're in college it will be time enough."
In my quiet way I never have cared much for horse shit so I
        went into Buffalo to Otto Ulbrich's book
Shop, where John Myers, to whom the arts stand indebted, then
        worked as a clerk: "You look interesting:
Here's a copy of my new little magazine, *Upstate*." I bought
        my book and hitchhiked home. Hiding what
It was like from old book burner, my stepfather, was an easy
        trick: "I have to write a book report: it's
A story about poor people in Ireland. Dublin." "Probably
        stinks to high hell it's so filthy. Here,
Let me see that book": he leafed through it, not knowing where
        to look for Molly Bloom, and tossed it at me:
"Still can't catch: go mow the lawn": I mowed the lawn. One
        day in American history class—taught by Miss
Pratt, so old in 1940 she still wore her hair in a pompadour,
        combed up over a rat—I was deep in the clotted
Irish rhetoric (as Frank O'Hara said about Dylan Thomas, "I can't
        stand all that Welsh spit") when a member of the
Football team leaned over: "That's the book that tells it like
        it is: it is hot—how did *you* get hold of it?"
"I guess the same way you did": bright and sassy: but to be
        spoken to by a football player and on equal

Terms! and the shock that anyone would think I was reading it
    as porn! This was art, this was truth, this
Was beauty: it was also laborious and dull, but I plowed on.
    When I first knew John Ashbery he slipped me
One of his trick test questions (we were looking at a window
    full of knitted ribbon dresses): "I don't think
James Joyce is any good: do you?" Think, what did I think! I
    didn't know you were *allowed* not to like James
Joyce. The book I suppose is a masterpiece: freedom of choice
    is better. Thank you, "Little J.A. in a
Prospect of Flowers." Last evening Mike mowed the lawn again:
    in the silken dawn each leaf and blade and
Needle bore its crystal drop, diamonds cut into pearl-shaped
    perfect globes (I never have seen a round
Diamond: why not? I'd like a few to rattle in my pocket: a
    change from rattling change), and the silk
Grew worn, and strained and frayed away and sister sun sipped
    the droplets up, not all at once, nor one at
A time, a steady vanishing into the air, sweetening, freshening,
    endewing the day. The days go by like leaves
That fall in fall, not yet, soon, so soon, I feel my death in
    currents of damp air on the back of my neck,
Filtered through a window screen (a casement window screen I
    open in the watches of the night, too lazy
To make it to the john, and take a moonlit piss into the Taxus),
    death, my death, over fifty years and that is
What I am building toward. No cremation, thanks, worm food,
    soil enrichment, mulch. Another morning and
I hand you a hammered silver brooch dripping wet, fished from a
    stream. Like a curse in a Greek myth, water,

Not rain in drops or streams, in sheets, water solid as that in
        a swimming pool, massively falls, bending the
Thick-stemmed orange lilies to the ground, turning overmown
        grass back from scorched tan to succulent green,
Curling (I've never noticed this before) maple leaves in on
        themselves like cupped hands and disclosing
Coral petioles: that one red leaf burns on in rain. Here is
        a story about Fairfield Porter. A long long
Time ago he went to paint in "the fairy woods" beyond the
        Double Beaches on Great Spruce Head Island.
He had his portable easel and was wearing, oh, sneakers, shorts,
        a shirt, and a straw hat, a farmer's hat. He
Set up shop and got to work: a view of Bear Island (owned by
        Buckminster Fuller and his sister Rosie). It
Was a fine hot day so Fairfield took off his clothes to enjoy
        what salty breeze there was and went on smearing
Maroger medium on his canvas. From Bear Island put out a rowboat
        or a canoe (I can't remember everything), in
It a couple, a man and a woman, rowing or paddling over the sunny
        bouncing water to the rocky point beyond where
He was painting. Fairfield thought of dressing, but on second
        thought reflected, "This *is* my island." Now he
Was working the pigments into the medium. The couple beached in
        a coign of the rocks, took ashore their lunch
Hamper, and took off their clothes. They were under forty and
        handsomely built. They ate their lunch, basked
In the sun and Fairfield forgot them as he went on painting.
        After a rest, the stranger got up and left
His mate to wander into "the fairy woods" (so named by Fairfield's
        German governess when he was a child: because

Of the silvery beards of moss that hung from the spruce), picking
        and eating wild raspberries that flourish there.
He looked up and the naked men confronted each other. Nobody
        said "Hello," "Goodbye," "Fine day" or "What's
Your name?" He went back to his woman, they dressed and returned
        to Bear Island over the broken gleaming water
Where seals snort and play. Our painter, in his farmer's hat,
        naked as a snake—to quote William Faulkner—
Finished his painting, dressed and ankled home. A winter or two
        later, in brash New York at a party, Fairfield
Noticed a man across the room who kept frowning at him. The frown
        broke into a smile, the smile broke into a grin.
The man pointed at him: "I know you: *you're the man in the hat!*"
        I wish I could say they went on to become the
Best of friends: they didn't, though I suppose they chatted:
        "How's Buckie? How's Rosie?" The painting?
The painting did not turn out one of the best. I think Kenneth
        Koch has it now. Fairfield's life was full of
Incidents like that, and he always carried them off with aplomb.
        Like the time he was canoeing naked and guess
What got sunburned. I like to think of sunburn on a day like
        today, rain in sheets and thunderclaps and
Lightning bolts: in the house the lights flicker on and off:
        we may go up in a sheet of flame: would the
Rain put it out? Who knows? I wish I were paddling an Old Town
        canoe with red and peeling shoulders, bouncing
Over and cutting through curling and icy water: fluent below
        me the giant seaweed called devil's-apron,
While there in the pebbly shallows off Landing Beach John Ashbery
        gathers mussels to scour and beard with a wire

Brush and an oyster knife, to steam and serve hot in soup plates,
     rich with the salts of the sea. "Do you often
Experience déjà vu, Jimmy?" Edwin asked me. "Why yes," I said
     (old Truthful Thomas). He and George exchanged
A look like a nod, "That proves it," it seemed to say. A lot of
     people believe that a proneness to déjà vu, that
Strange and not unwonderful feeling, I have experienced this, this
     light, these trees, these birds, heard the very
Words you are saying, before, or, it all clicks into place and
     I know what you are about to say: "Please
Stop picking your nose": there, you said it: they see this as
     a definite symptom of schizophrenia. Hence
the look between wise old Edwin (the color of silvery parchment)
     and knowing George (whose looks were beginning
To go: it wasn't déjà vu that told me they both were hung like
     stallions: only a slight case of experience):
I was feeling upset enough God knows, the sanatorium door stood
     agape: but I subscribe to a simpler explanation:
One lobe of the brain registers the event, what in simple reality
     is said or happens or is seen, while the other
Lobe takes it in a split second, an infinitesimal split second
     later, so, in a sense, there is a real déjà vu,
Half the brain has experienced the experience: "I have been here
     before": you have: so know-it-all George and
Edwin can go screw themselves with stalks of glass wheat. Like
     my dream this morning, casting a pall over
This part of the day (why did it have to stop raining?): Donald
     and Roy exchanged a sharp glance, it meant,
"Jimmy is going over the hill": I left in pique and took the
     funicular down the sandstone cliffs: on either

Side businessmen in hats and carrying briefcases were sucking
　　　　each other off in cave-like cubicles: on
The sunless beach, the day after a storm with screaming and
　　　　wheeling gulls and flotsam and jetsam, boards
Stuck with bent and rusty nails and wound with bladder wrack,
　　　　they—the border patrol, the cops, the fuzz—
Stopped me and asked to see my passport: in my mind I could
　　　　see it in a desk drawer in an orange room:
In this land you can't forget your passport: I turned and left
　　　　them and they let me go: I climbed the gritty
Steps which soon penetrated the cliff, the rear entrance to a
　　　　horrible apartment house in the Bronx: to
Go forward could only get worse: I turned and ran back down
　　　　to where the tunnel issued from the cliff:
Below me boys were gathering rocks on the beach with which to
　　　　stone me. I woke up, glad to get out of my
Fresh white bed (usually, I would rather sleep than do anything):
　　　　why should a dream like that fill me with gloom,
A kind of moral hangover: "I may want to die, but at least I
　　　　am still alive?" Was it only yesterday I
Awoke to streaming rain from a dream, a vision, like a late painting
　　　　of Fairfield's, one of the ones of a misshapen
Sun burning through mist over a sliding morning sea? There is
　　　　only one sky: a pewter plate, easily bent:
There are two windows: out one grass may be damp but looks dry;
　　　　out the one to the east, enclosed by trees, the
Broad and pointed leaves of Solomon's-seal are thickly set with
　　　　water drops, as easy to gather as colorless wild
Berries in a cleft in a cliff, as beads on a Patou dance frock:
　　　　green barely freaked with blue and glitter:

Japanese lanterns and serpentine, a confetti blizzard, New Year's
       Eve on a ship at sea, Isham Jones, the Coon Sanders
Band: "And now for your pleasure, ladies and gentlemen, Miss Irene
       Bordoni." Or was it Fifi D'Orsay? Last night,
Driving to the Old Orchard Inn, a flash flood. "Why would a bank,"
       my brother asked, "be crazy enough to finance a
House on the flat by a creek where the cellar is bound to flood
       whenever it rains?" Why, indeed? Crossing
Cazenovia Creek the smoothly racing water was almost up to the
       bridge, silent, smooth and creased, a tossed-
Out length of coffee-colored satin. Sadistically, I hoped to
       see a drowned Holstein floating by, a ship of
Furry flesh, its udder like a motor. Drowned Holstein eyes; but
       not a Jersey. None.

            A better morning comes to pass
            Sunlight buttered on the grass
            Late, late, I lie awake
            Finding pleasure for its own sake
            Reading books to pass the time
            Print on paper, algae, slime
            Until before the dawn a gray
            Light breaks, will the day be gay
            Or will thunder-stones roll this way?
            The former, yes, it may turn out,
            Though, no, the latter still come about.
            In jinglejangle the day may pass
            Light freshly buttered on the grass.
My mother goes off to the podiatrist: she has an ingrown toe-
       nail, it's turning black and looks infected

To me. My sister-in-law will drive. It hurt so much yesterday
        morning (Sunday) she almost didn't go to church:
An unheard-of thing. Every weekend we have the same talk:
        "Jim, wouldn't you like to come to church?"
Sometimes I'm rude and say, "Lay off!" Mostly I manage a polite,
        "No thank you." "I wish you would." "If
wishes were horses then beggars could ride. In other words, I'm
        not going to church." "I wouldn't object if you
Want to go to the Catholic church." "If I wanted to go to the
        Catholic church, then I would go. As it happens
I don't." Then why do I carry a rosary with me? Partly because
        a half-mad old woman gave me one (I have two,
As it happens). "You look like a good boy," she said, "here, take
        this": a handful of beads and a dangling crucifix.
I remember the beads slipping through my fingers, decade after decade,
        as the car spun east through Newport, the luxury
Cottages, the cliffs, the sea: what happened to what I thought
        were my resolutions, praying in the Lady Chapel
At St. Patrick's, going to mass with kindly, jolly Father Lynch,
        attending a lecture by Karl Stern, the
Catholic psychiatrist? That was a turn-off: his idea of sin
        was certainly not mine: I have never been
Sure about sin: wrong, yes, but sin and evil, it all gets too
        glib, too easy. Then meeting the head of Fordham,
Like a handsome snake with George Raft hair (only silvery) who gave
        me the fish eye: except for Father Lynch, I can
Live without Jesuits. I can live, it seems, without religion,
        though I have never wanted to. Brush in hand,
You've slipped out of my poem: I have such confidence in your
        future, in what you'll create, with paint and

Canvas, Conté crayon and heavy paper, views, faces, a pier glass
    in a long room, a fence hung with roses out a
Garden window: is the stereo playing, and if so, what? *The Ring,*
    Scriabin, moth-wing strokes of Sviatoslav Richter's
Steady fingers? Here, I have no phonograph: television. My mother
    watches (i.e., dozes off) while I sit and read.
The Olympics were fun, marvelous slow-motion underwater shots,
    replays, of swimmers' arms and shoulders
Flexing and pulling and the turn and push off the wall, the
    high divers leaping and spinning to straighten
And cut the water like the blade of a knife; the gymnasts, the
    fourteen-year-old girl from Roumania who could do
Anything, anything she pleased, delightful, enchanting, and how
    the crowd went wild when the Russian weight
Lifter broke the Olympic record and then came back to break all
    other existing records: "He's the strongest
Man in the world!" the announcer squealed. "Ladies and gentlemen,
    you've just seen him: the world's strongest
Man!" His voice broke in his excitement. Then horses and hurdles
    and Princess Anne: her horse was too feisty to
Handle: the royal family decorated a box: the Queen, Prince
    Philip, the Prince of Wales, his brothers: a
Close-up shot: my mother came to long enough to ask, "Does the
    Queen have any children?" And dozed off again.
I switch to *Mod Squad*: Adam Greer (played by Tige Andrews) is
    being shot by almost invisible poison pellets:
He passes out on the grass: will Peggy Lipton and Clarence
    Williams III find out what the poison is in
Time to obtain an antidote? It seems likely. But what *are* you
    painting, oh you who paint on West 22nd Street?

You're not much of one for writing letters, are you? But then,
    you said you weren't so I can't complain. No
More am I. A bundle of postcards, all of them dull, sits and has
    sat on this desk for days. This afternoon I must
Mail them to you. But it looks like rain! Not again! I wish
    I could send you a bundle of orange lilies
To paint. They stand—and lean—in a row, at the top of a wall
    by the drive. Their anthers are so delicately
Hung that just walking past makes them swing, and if they brush
    your clothes they leave dark brown stains. Wake up
In the night, after midnight, and open the casement screen and
    study the road gliding downhill, brightly
Lighted by a misshapen half moon, almost white, scooped out of
    lemon ice. How can macadam (or is it called
Asphalt or blacktop?) return this lunar light as a river or
    creek might? On this quiet small-town street,
Whose car coasts quietly up the hill at this late hour? Returning
    from a social event? A night worker going home
To bed? Haven't I seen this car at this hour before? About
    now Mr Talbot used to drive home from the
Buffalo paper for which he wrote a nature column, hunting and
    fishing, the ways of wildlife and what was and
Wasn't burgeoning in fields and swamps. And a little later Joe
    Palmer's sedan slid by, also home from a Buffalo
Paper, a different paper, a rewrite man. Other people live in
    their houses: I know a lot of dead people: I
Don't think of them much. Standing at the window, staring at the
    street, staring at the tree behind which swiftly
Slips the bright twist of a demi-moon, I wish for someone to take
    a nocturnal stroll with, like the moonless

Night on Great South Beach when the waves broke and sprayed us
        and you put your arm around my shoulders and
I thought, why can't we walk on like this forever? Sandy sneakers.
        A car (called the Green Bomb), a drive, home, a
Shower, mussed sheets, bed, sleep as total black at four windows
        melted into the false dawn. Sleep into sunshine,
A Cranshaw melon, and you drive away. I'm chilled at this window
        here in western New York, studying and losing
What's left of the moon: tomorrow night there'll be a bigger
        serving. An August morning, cool and cloudless,
Maple leaves lightly moving, conifers perfectly still, robins
        skimming the grass where a fat black dog named
Cornelia just took a dump, a sky not blue but white, up the valley
        from Olean a freight train passes (the distant
Sound of breakers), down the valley toward Olean the loudness and
        smell of diesel trucks, children's voices: shrill:
Back-yard swimming-pool voices. One train rolling toward Buffalo
        right after the other: that's rare: it's
Raining not knowing why. You put down your brush and sit down and
        stare at what you've painted. You light a mild
Cigarette, or a thin cigar. Whoever knows what a painter is thinking?
        Is it obscure and muggy in Chelsea, or light and
Shivery the way it is here? What shall I do with the rest of
        the morning? Shower, shave, write to Barbara,
Go uptown and buy cool milk in waxy cartons? Call my nephew
        and go for a walk? Try to remember what I
Forgot? What I can't remember is the name of my New York doctor:
        "Murray." But Murray what? I must have it
Written down some place, and if I haven't "you" can tell me.
        When you read this poem you will have to decide

Which of the "yous" are "you." I think you will have no trouble,
      as you rise from your chair and take up your
Brush again and scrub in some green, that particular green,
      whose name I can't remember. Thank God the
Sky cleared: I think it is tonight that the moon is full! Round
      and white as opaque ice, hung from a sky hook
Over a city avenue, tonight, riding slowly up a rural sky, a wheel
      of Gourmandise with the foil peeled off, smelling
Sweetly of cherries, the colorless side of a Royal Anne cherry,
      shedding light perhaps, perhaps with a ring on
The blue-serge night: does a ring around the moon portend rain?
      I bet it does, I bet it will, this dank and
Somber summer. The screen through which I peer cubes all into
      sampler stitches: the suppertime shadows laid
Out in topiary work, a dolphin, a spire, a dog, your name, flat
      and roughly clipped, dark on light, dark green
On bright moon green, the world smells of mown grass. I think
      I see a mountain it must be a cloud: there is
No mountain. Let there be a mountain: Why not? Didn't Long
      Island have a hurricane last night? Didn't
I long to be there in the four-poster bed and hear the shutters
      rattle and the windowpanes whistle and sing
And the thunder of the surf, wind in the giant plane tree? And
      to get up in a cleared-off day and go to the beach
And the dunes and see the scattered wrack, fish and weed and
      (always) some cast-up surprise: fishing
Gear, net, an ominous object of red and orange plastic, breakers
      rough, dull and full of sand and the sinus-
Clearing oceanic smell. Dunes carved into new shapes, salt
      air, combing through the cut grass, beach plum,

Unkillable rosa rugosa. Maybe a big beach cottage has had its
       foundation of sand eroded by water and wind:
Toppling, ready to tumble: why so much pleasure in wrack and
       ruin? A house falls into the sea: my heart
Gives a jump. But the paper says the eye of the hurricane and
       the moon-drawn high of the tide did not coincide:
Probably nothing much happened. What a gyp. Or better this way?
       at least I needn't feel guilty for my pleasure
In wrack and ruin. Suppertime shadows sneaking over the lawn,
       a buzz saw slicing a tree into portions, cars
Coming up the hill to dinner (they all eat Jell-O), me smoking
       and you painting: no: cleaning your brushes
(Though about that you are not quite so scrupulous as some I
       know): what's for dinner? Shrimp croquettes?
Barbara Guest sent me a card, "Architectural Perspective, Italian,
       late 15th Century," that gave me a pang, that makes
Me long to take you to that loveliest land and we could visit
       Vicenza, walk up the drive to the Villa
Rotunda, the building with the noblest profile in the world,
       see the cut of the flights of steps as you
Slowly perambulate through grass scattered with pecking white
       chickens, go to the hilltop wall and look
Down at the fields below, where peacocks fan their tails. I doubt
       it will happen: still, there's our projected trip
To Washington and the National Gallery, that's to look forward to.
       Paintings are such a pleasure: can I tempt you
With Cleveland and Boston and Baltimore? California, frankly,
       is just too far. Suppertime shadows, my gastric
Juices are beginning to flow. Barbara writes, "I can see you working
       & poking your head outdoors in the evening—or

Taking a late walk—" she may be right. She was right, I poked
     my head out of doors after supper (beef in
Tomato sauce—ick) and there the tiger lilies were, in a row
     above a low wall above the drive in which grew
A few more tiger lilies, reddish orange, petals turning back,
     dark brown pollen, no scent, the strong
Thick stems beaded with round black seeds. Further on, past
     the birdbath, its basin partly filled with
Cunk (childhood memory: "Put down that book and go scrub the
     birdbath"), to the apple and quince trees
Looking so old, so unkempt: I remember planting them, they were
     just seedlings, or do I mean saplings? Now
They stand, unpruned, unbearing, smothered in swags of Concord
     grape leaves lightly, heavily moving like the
Heave of the sea, leaf over leaf, and hung among them cloudy
     green bunches of grapes. I would like to wait
And see them empurple, I would like to wait and taste that particular
     taste, so sweet when they're really ripe: did
They tell you that if you swallow them the seeds will catch in
     your appendix and give you peritonitis? I
Always swallow them, don't you? Letting the oozy grape meat slide
     down my throat like an oyster: grapes, oysters
And champagne: bliss is such a simple thing. A faded photograph
     shows (it says in pencil on the back), "This is
What the woods are like": white-stemmed trees, smudges (needles),
     rough soft grass. (I made limeade: sticky
Fingers: I drink and type: sticky keys.) Those woods, that
     island and the bay, I won't forget them soon,
Nor that same moon I saw last night hang in glory over this small
     hill I used to see ride, embosomed, in the fullness

Of the sky it lit etching the tall, still spruce and casting its
        light on the rippled water that led off and off
To ocean and to where you cannot see: to go out through the
        dining porch among the daisies and the crags
And moon-bathe. Have you ever swum at night in water so cold it's
        like plunging into a case of knives, your quickly
Moving limbs dripping with moonstones, liquid moonstones? I turned
        my back and this small green world went shadowless:
The nimbus is back at four in the afternoon: no moon tonight. Before
        dawn I woke and made my oatmeal, orange juice and
Coffee and thought how this poem seems mostly about what I've lost:
        the one who mattered most, my best friend, Paul
(Who mattered least), the Island, the California wild-flower paper,
        the this, the that, Whippoorwill, buried friends,
And the things I only write between the lines. What can one write
        between the lines? Not one damn thing. Look over
Your shoulder, into the future: one thing I want to see is heavy
        snow falling in Chelsea, to walk in it, snow
Blowing in my face, from where I live to where you live, to stomp
        the snow off in your vestibule, to punch your bell,
To hear the buzzer buzz, to push the door and see the open inside
        door and you smiling there: "Hi-ee: how *are*
You? What will it be? The usual?" A tall cold glass of Vichy.
        Winter in New York, when the big wet flakes
Stream horizontal. (Funny, I haven't beat my meat in days—why's
        that?) I think it may rain again tonight—a
Shower, a smattering—suddenly I feel it in the breeze that
        lifts the paper on which I type. I smell
It, faintly, the fresh faint smell of coming summer rain. I
        used to climb out my first-floor bedroom

Window, naked, into it: the slippery wet bathmat grass, the
 rain, both cool and warm, plastering down
My hair, rain running all over me as I danced or stood in it,
 the long persistent tongues of summer rain:
"Want a trip around the world?" "O.K." And so it did, the
 licking, bathing summer rain. Another dawn as
Gray as hands that shovel pea coal into an Aga cookstove: under
 it, the walks and road shine slick as though
Greased with Vaseline: in the middle of the night, deep in
 the dark of that time of the morning when it
Seems light will never return and only a weight of black go on
 and on, what a storm we had, the lancing of the
Rain, the thunder cracks and lightning bolts happening as one: I
 thought the house was struck, or at least a
Nearby tree, my bedroom lighting up in flares like the strobe
 light in a discotheque. You bet I didn't go out
In that for any sexy rain bath: no-siree-bob. The air is cool
 but heavy, clammy, robins are garnering earth-
Worms from the lawn: I see one long worm wriggle as it's swallowed.
 Early, so early, it lightly rains again: or is
It drops showering down from leaves on other leaves? So early
 that the morning paper hasn't come yet: Eric
Larsen brings it, he's about thirteen, with yellow Scandinavian
 hair: first his older brother passes, with
Papers for houses further up the hill, then, at, oh, seven or
 so, Eric trudges across the grass to leave the
Courier Express on the brick steps: "Good morning, Eric," "Good
 morning," gruff, but with a shy smile, and I
Sit down to coffee and the news: the Republican Convention, rapes
 and muggings, arson: arson—I don't know why—

Is very big on the Niagara Frontier. A barn burner has been busy
      on these summer nights: the *Courier* keeps
Pointing out he doesn't seem to want to hurt anybody, he just
      wants to see the wood flame and roar up into
The night sky (although one herd of Holsteins were roasted in
      their stalls: perhaps our friend didn't know
That they were there?): I'm glad his meat is not small white clapboard
      houses. A day comes in a month, in a season, and
You wish it were some other month, another season. I never have
      liked August much, I wish it were September,
October, I wish it were the fall. Falling leaves, glittering
      blue skies, in the country, late goldenrod
And asters, in the city, a crackle to the air, a crackle, and
      at the same time a balminess. The Bluebird
Laundry truck comes and goes (I missed my chat with the freckled
      driver), there are small dandelions scattered
On the lawn: no, yellowed Euonymus leaves blown down by last
      night's storm. With all that sudden force, not
A single lily stalk was bent or broken. They stand in rows in
      metal strength and curve their petals back
And give a point to August. "All he cares about are leaves and
      flowers and weather": and who are you, which
Maple are you I mean, the one who curves its leaves like hands,
      disclosing pink palms growing in clusters on
Branches with silver bark and already bearing five, six, colored
      (a light rich red) leaves? A silver bark?
A swamp maple: isn't that the one whose leaves turn first? I
      think it is, I remember one, deeply blazing
Full in late summer, growing in swampy ground where the waterfall
      tumbled and tinkled down to feed the beaver pond.

The other evening my mother and I were watching TV in the living
       room when something fell, a metal clang on the
Back stoop. I went and put the outside lights on and looked:
       the trash-can lid had been knocked off and
Perched on the can full of trash was the biggest raccoon I've
       ever seen: he turned his head and looked me
In the eye, hopped down and walked sedately off into the shrubs.
       I put the lid back on and dragged the can into
The vestibule. "I wish you had seen him," I told my mother, "he
       was beautiful: he was so *big!*" "Maybe he
Was a dog," she said, deep in her TV program. I don't know why,
       but that breaks me up, like telling someone
You've seen a rat, and they say, "Maybe it was a fat mouse."
       I'd love to have picked him up and held him,
Only, frankly, I thought he might incline to bite. I would like
       to put food out for him, but how could I know
He was eating it and not the dogs that swarm around this hill?
       The dogs, they get enough to eat at home.
The mail comes, the mailman smiles and goes away in blue, slowly
       and steadily, to the next house behind a screen
Of trees and shrubs (spruce, forsythia). Letters from Kenward,
       Trevor, Anne Porter, Darragh and "Domaine de St.
Esteve, Lambesc," in other words, Anne Dunn, who writes:

     It was nice having the Hazans here but unfortunately I had to
     leave midway through their visit as my brother was dying and I
     wanted to be with him. In so far as dying of cancer is bearable
     his death was, his wife, two daughters and myself never left him,
     until the last 24 hours the grandchildren and the dogs ran in and
     out as usual, he was heavily doped but conscious and felt reas-
     sured by our being there. I must admit his dying was pretty

harrowing, I have never sat holding someone's hand before as they "take off." After the funeral Rodrigo and I went to Lincoln to see the cathedral which was one of Philip's last wishes so we filled in for him, on the way there we went to the Peak District which was beautiful, rolling country flecked with stone walls and dreamy cows, we stayed at Bakewell and ate Bakewell tarts, also visited Chatsworth Gardens which are sensational and put the Himalayas to shame, the scale is so cunningly manipulated, extraordinary growths of giant cow parsley by rushing streams, I wish you had been there. The temperature was in the 90's which you wouldn't have liked much. I fell in love with the Lincolnshire wolds. We came back by the Boston Stump (St. Botolph's) restored by the good people of Boston, Mass, and Ely whose cathedral I really loved, much more so than Lincoln.

How English, the children and the dogs—especially the dogs—
    running in and out of the room where the man—
The son, brother, husband, father, grandfather—lay slowly dying.
    "In the midst of life we are in death, in the
Midst of death we are in life": I know how harrowing it must
    have been for you, but, though I'm not much of
A mystic, I'm sure in that long last handclasp he gave you something:
    not just love, the electric flow of his failing
Power: a gentle charge: and in exchange took with him from your
    physical grip all that you felt for him all those
Years, condensed in a red pulsation. And what a fine memorial, to
    take a pleasant pilgrimage he would have liked to
Take: Lincoln, the Lincolnshire wolds, the Peak District, Ely, the
    gardens at Chatsworth (Paxton, surely?): yes,
I wish I had been with you. Perhaps one day I will. Dear, dear
    Anne. What is "the Isle of Ely"? Is there

Really an island? And when next you come to 185 East 85th, please
  bake me a Bakewell tart: I'm sure there's a
Recipe in that Florence White cookbook I gave you (and I would
  not mind a Grassy Corner pudding). Here,
Stillness, and a car honks twice, lunchtime stillness: all
  morning we lived in a barbershop, the
Perpetual power mowers shaving away the relentlessly growing
  grass. Peace and quiet, a sullen, sultry sun
Slants under a leaden sky. A fat woman in a loose dress pads
  down the hill: who's she? A big white
Butterfly zigzags by, and a smaller yellow one: distantly,
  a dog barks, nearby, a young child yammers
And squawks (the neighbors have children and grandchildren
  visiting), I subside into the quiet of my
Room, annunciated by the rapid ticking of my cheap alarm clock.
  (The phone bill came: last month I spent
A hundred dollars on long-distance calls: I must be bored here,
  without my friends: I shouldn't do it, but
Calling France is so much fun: "Give me the overseas operator":
  oh to be rich, to do all you want, to visit
Chatsworth and Bathurst, in New Brunswick: oh, you know.) August
  half over, and another dawn that is no dawn, a
Mezzotint of a morning: how I used to pore over Pennell's *Etchers
  and Etching*, plate after plate, weird, smeared,
Sooty, scratched: Rembrandt, Whistler, Goya, Félicien Rops, an
  Irishman whose name I forget, a stream densely
Banked by unmown grass: water, sunlight, succulence, a curve.
  I'd like to collect etchings of the post-Whistler
Period, minor works by minor masters, evocative and fresh. My
  heavy naked calves are etched with hairs, worn

Off on the inner side where my legs rub against my jeans. On
      this miserable Sunday morning ("Jim, are you
Sure you wouldn't like to come to church?") I like to sit in this
      Hitchcock chair and idly pull my foreskin—I'm
Sitting in my undershorts—and drink iced tea and smoke and have
      a passing sexy thought for someone I won't ever
Have—the eyes, the wide slope of the shoulders, the thighs—and
      let tunes play in my head: Carly Simon singing
"Anticipation," Mado Robin singing "Fascination," golden oldies.
      I have a friend who when he wakes up in the
Morning likes to just lie there and feel himself all over (maybe
      he's afraid he vanished in the night: I rather
Wish he would): I like to lie in bed at night and read and feel
      myself, shoulders, armpits, chest, belly, crotch,
And maybe tweak a hair. Once I found a kind of a swarm of moles
      on my rib cage—only I don't think they were
Moles: I don't know what they were, not scabies, not a rash: little
      lumps, growths, a colony. I put rubbing alcohol on
Them and in a few days they were gone. I don't like any funny business,
      stuff like that. Herpes simplex! That's a drag:
Eye salve is good for it, I found that out from a doc in Zurich where
      I stayed in a snow-white hotel beside the glassy green
And rushing river on which swans pointed upstream toward the bridge
      on whose balustrade I was drunkenly leaning one
January night when some men came by and spoke to me in German:
      "Surely you speak English?" I said: they thought
I was a gas. We went somewhere to drink and soon I was in bed with
      a supple, gray-haired man, playing snakes, flailing
About and knocking the bedside lamp on the floor. He ran one of
      the big hotels and used to send me packets of

Marrons glacés sprinkled with candied violets: the desk clerk
        began to give me funny looks when he handed me
My daily tribute. How I gobbled them up! I wonder what my chum's
        name was? Once, when we were having dinner, the
String quartet played "Wien, Wien," and he leaned across the table
        and took my hand and said, "This will be our team
Song": it took a while to figure out what he meant. And once he
        said, "Come here": we stepped into his bathroom,
He picked a razor up and shaved my sideburns off. What crust. I
        didn't really mind though: I'd only grown them
Because what else do you do on a nine-day crossing? What I did
        mind was that it emerged he was a major bore, so
I packed my duds and took an express train to Geneva, which I only
        went to because I wanted to stay at a hotel where
Henry James had stayed: it had fallen on sorry days and my view of
        Lake Leman was one of banks of fog. I walked past
Calvin's house on moist cobbles, bought a volume of Gide's diary,
        saw George Raft in *Scarface*, and took the train
To Italy, passing the inspiration of Byron's "The Prisoner of
        Chillon." Switzerland, so long. July is gone,
A hunk of August, a few blank days got lost (I couldn't stop sleeping),
        the sun came back in cloudlessness, hot yesterday,
Hotter today, hotter still tomorrow the TV set predicts: shower
        baths help: I'm well bedewed this minute, my
Hair slicked down, and icy orange juice and iced tea with lemon—
        both are on my desk—no wonder my time is spent
Hanging out over the toilet, splashing away like a mountain meadow
        rill. Late in the afternoon and suddenly a cool
Breeze springs up and streams in the window: the leaves shudder:
        how sweet, when something you really enjoy

Unexpectedly arrives, like the postcard I got this morning from
      Ned Rorem, with flattering words about some of my
Poems, how kind, how nice, but I'm glad I'm not with him on Nantucket,
      where I got one of the worst sunburns of my life—
I wonder what it's like, being a composer? Writing goes by so fast:
      a couple of hours of concentration, then you're
Spent: but music takes so much time: the sounds come into your
      head, but then, the writing them down, the little
Notes. I can see Nantucket now, sand and whipping grass under a
      glare of sun. There are not many islands I really
Like, the ones where the rocks are slithery under the
      thick seaweed when the tide is out, where the
Heart of the island beneath tall trees is all overgrown with ferns
      and moss begemmed with fog and is silent, spongy
To walk on: on other days, a scented springy mattress to stretch
      out on. Little boats emerge from behind other
Islands: utter peace and total privacy. Still, Nantucket has its
      points, but I prefer to go north and further north:
Maine, New Brunswick, Nova Scotia. Oh, what's to make such a fuss
      about? I like all sorts of places. I can't
Believe it, I have to go piss again: it's like that night in
      Paris when I first got bombed on Pernod: I
Was making my way along the boulevard back to the hotel when my
      bladder flashed the message that I had to go and
I had to go *now*, not in two minutes: up ahead, in the same block,
      I could see a pissoir (I mean, a *vespasienne*)
But that just wasn't close enough, nor could l run. I plunged my
      left hand in my pocket, and got a good grip, like
Stopping the flow in a hose, and walked stiff-legged along: the
      pressure, the pain, was something else: "My

Brow was wet": I made it: there I was, confronting a urinal: I
       inched down my zipper and put my right hand into
The opening: hideous trauma, there was just no way I could transfer
       my swollen tool from hand to hand without a great
Gushing forth (inside my pants), like when Moses hit the rock: so
       I did it: there was piss all over Paris, not
To mention my shirt and pants, light sun tans: why couldn't it
       have been the depths of winter, and me in heavy
Dark overcoat? I was so mad I stomped on my way, thinking, "Well
       if somebody wants to make something out of it . . ."
(Young and dumb, it never occurred to me that if I'd spilled a
       drink in a café, I'd have looked the same.)
But Pernod, Pernod is murder. I wish I had some now, but tea
       and orange juice will have to do:
Tomorrow: New York: in blue, in green, in white, East Aurora
       goodbye.

Printed in the USA
CPSIA information can be obtained
at www.ICGtesting.com
LVHW091136150724
785511LV00001B/174